Prime Ministers of Canada

Turn of the 20th Century

By Bev Cline

Weigl

CALGARY
www.weigl.com

Published by Weigl Educational Publishers Limited
6325 10 Street SE
Calgary, Alberta, Canada
T2H 2Z9

Website: www.weigl.com

Library and Archives Canada Cataloguing in Publication

Cline, Beverly Fink, 1951-
        The new nation / Beverly Cline.
(Prime ministers of Canada)
Includes index.
ISBN 1-55388-247-4 (bound).--ISBN 1-55388-246-6 (pbk.)
        1. Prime ministers--Canada--Biography--Juvenile literature.
2. Canada--History--1867-1914--Juvenile literature. I. Title.
II. Series: Prime ministers of Canada (Calgary, Alta.)
FC26.P7C63 2006   j971.009'9   C2006-902474-X

Printed in Canada
1 2 3 4 5 6 7 8 9 0 10 09 08 07 06

Cover: Sir Robert Borden served as Canada's prime minister through the entirety of World War I.

Photo Credits: Glenbow Museum Archives: pages 5 (nc-6-11899), 14 (NA-404-1), 33 (NA-1959-1); **Courtesy of Heather Hudak:** page 30; **Library and Archives Canada:** pages 4 (C-005327, C-010460, PA-033933, C-001971), 5 (C-00687, PA-128175), 9 (PA-025601), 16 (C-016715) 34 (C-000242), 35 (PA-030212), 36 (PA-025025), 37 (PA-163001), 41 top (C-0006940; 44 (C-087137, C-095730); **Saskatchewan Archives:** page 4 (R-D700); **Reproduction courtesy of Windsor's Community Museum:** page 32 (P6110).

Every reasonable effort has been made to trace ownership and to obtain permission to reprint copyright material. The publishers would be pleased to have any errors or omissions brought to their attention so that they may be corrected in subsequent printings.

We acknowledge the financial support of the Government of Canada through the Book Publishing Industry Development Program (BPIDP) for our publishing activities.

Project Coordinator
Tatiana Tomljanovic

Design
Terry Paulhus

All of the Internet URLs given in the book were valid at the time of publication. However, due to the dynamic nature of the Internet, some addresses may have changed, or sites may have ceased to exist since publication. While the author and publisher regret any inconvenience this may cause readers, no responsibility for any such changes can be accepted by either the author or the publisher.

Contents

Canada's Prime Ministers

Since **Confederation**, there have been 22 Canadian prime ministers. Canada's prime ministers have come from many provinces and cultures. Some of them, such as the first prime minister, John A. Macdonald, were born in other countries. They came to Canada because they, or their parents, decided Canada was the best place to live and raise a family.

Canada's prime ministers are people of many talents and different interests. Some trained as lawyers, while others were journalists, doctors, farmers, writers, teachers, business people, and members of the **civil service**. Some of them fought as soldiers to protect Canada and her allies. All of them had one thing in common. They wanted to make Canada one of the best places in the world to live.

THE NEW NATION (CONFEDERATION TO 1896)

 John A. Macdonald
(July 1, 1867–November 5, 1873; October 17, 1878–June 6, 1891)

 Alexander Mackenzie
(November 7, 1873–October 8, 1878)

 John J. C. Abbott
(June 16, 1891–November 24, 1892)

 John S. D. Thompson
(December 5, 1892–December 12, 1894)

 Mackenzie Bowell
(December 21, 1894–April 27, 1896)

 Charles H. Tupper
(May 1, 1896–July 8, 1896)

TURN OF THE 20ᵀᴴ CENTURY (1896–1920)

 Wilfrid Laurier
(July 11, 1896–October 6, 1911)

 Robert L. Borden
(October 10, 1911–July 10, 1920)

TIME OF TURMOIL (1920–1948)

 Arthur Meighen
(July 10, 1920–December 29, 1921; June 29, 1926–September 25, 1926)

 Richard B. Bennett
(August 7, 1930–October 23, 1935)

 William Lyon Mackenzie King
(December 29, 1921–June 28, 1926; September 25, 1926–August 7, 1930; October 23, 1935–November 15, 1948)

TIME OF TRANSITION (1948–1968)

 Louis S. Saint Laurent
(November 15, 1948–June 21, 1957)

 John George Diefenbaker
(June 21, 1957–April 22, 1963)

 Lester B. Pearson
(April 22, 1963–April 20, 1968)

TRUDEAU ERA (1968–1984)

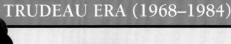

 Pierre Elliott Trudeau
(April 20, 1968–June 3, 1979; March 3, 1980–June 30, 1984)

 Charles Joseph Clark
(June 4, 1979–March 2, 1980)

 John N. Turner
(June 30, 1984–September 17, 1984)

CONTEMPORARY CANADA (1984 TO PRESENT)

 Martin Brian Mulroney
(September 17, 1984–June 13, 1993)

 Jean J. Chrétien
(October 25, 1993–December 12, 2003)

Kim Campbell
(June 13, 1993–October 25, 1993)

 Paul E. P. Martin
(December 12, 2003–February 6, 2006)

 Stephen J. Harper
(February 6, 2006–)

The New Century

The turn of the 20th century brought many challenges for Prime Ministers Laurier and Borden; perhaps the most difficult was trying to balance French and English interests.

With a population of 5.3 million in 1900, Canada had grown considerably since Confederation. As **immigrants** continued to pour into western Canada, farmers produced grains and dairy products in unsurpassed amounts. The factories in central Canada worked at maximum capacity producing pulp and paper, boots and shoes, agricultural implements, and **textiles**. The earth yielded rich quantities of copper, iron, coal, and nickel.

By the end of the 19ᵗʰ century, the world seemed much smaller than it had appeared only 30 years earlier. Steamships journeyed to all corners of the earth. Telephones provided instant communication throughout North America. In 1901, in St. John's, Newfoundland, the first trans-Atlantic wireless message was received. By the following year, an underwater cable connected Vancouver to Australia. Electric streetcars provided rapid, convenient transportation within the larger Canadian cities, and railways linked communities together.

This was an era of inventions and change. The motor car replaced the horse and buggy. The first airplane took flight in 1903. Other firsts included the motion picture camera, the safety razor, the typewriter, the electric stove, the cash register, and the electric vacuum cleaner.

There were, however, still some problems. Wealth was not shared equally. Workers and farmers wanted more influence in government. Women demanded political equality. The greatest challenge facing Prime Minster Wilfrid Laurier and his successor Robert Laird Borden at the turn of the century was balancing the desires of French and English Canada during World War I. Under the leadership of Laurier and Borden, Canada emerged as a full-fledged nation.

Wilfrid Laurier was the first French Canadian to become prime minister.

Keeping Canada Together

"If there is anything, to which I have given my political life...it is to try to promote unity, harmony, and amity between the diverse elements of this country."
Wilfrid Laurier on his efforts to balance English- and French-Canadian interests

Wilfrid Laurier: "The Great Conciliator"

"Canada has been modest in its history, although its history, in my estimation, is only commencing. It is commencing in this century. The nineteenth century was the century of the United States. I think we can claim that Canada will fill the twentieth century."
Laurier, January 18, 1904

Wilfrid Laurier became prime minister of Canada in 1896. He was full of optimism about the country's future. The economy was booming, and there was still plenty of room for farming to expand in the Prairies. The future looked bright.

Laurier's task over the next 15 years was not easy. Canada was changing, and these changes created divisions in society. Workers were asking why their wages were so low when their employers lived a life of luxury. Farmers in the West struggled to make a living from the land.

French Canadians worried that English Canadians were trying to prevent them from keeping their own language and culture. People questioned whether Canada should remain part of the British Empire if it meant it could not be independent. Fortunately, Laurier was both charming and **charismatic**. The first French Canadian to become prime minister, his captivating speeches and pleasant personality won people over. He was able to achieve agreement where none had existed before. As a result, he won the elections of 1900, 1904, and 1908. He lost the 1911 election to Robert Borden and the Conservative Party.

No prime minister served a longer continuous term than Sir Wilfrid Laurier.

Laurier's Early Years

Laurier was born in 1841. He grew up in Saint-Lin, Quebec, as the son of a farmer and rural surveyor. He was only seven years old when his mother died. His sister Malvina died when he was 14. Laurier's mother encouraged his love of books and music. When Laurier was 11, his father and grandfather decided he should live with a family in New Glasgow so that he could learn English. Two years later, he entered the College of L'Assomption to study literature, the classics, mathematics, and history. At school, he was a popular leader and became fascinated with politics and the law. At 19, Laurier went to study law at McGill University in Montreal. In 1867, he set up a law office in Arthabaska. Laurier won a seat as a federal member of **Parliament** in 1873. In 1887, Laurier became the Liberal Party leader. Nine years later, he became the first French-Canadian prime minister of Canada.

"The old charmer! He bamboozles me most sweetly often. I know he does it. And he knows I know. But he bamboozles me still which is the main thing."
One journalist in 1910 admitted he had fallen under Laurier's spell.

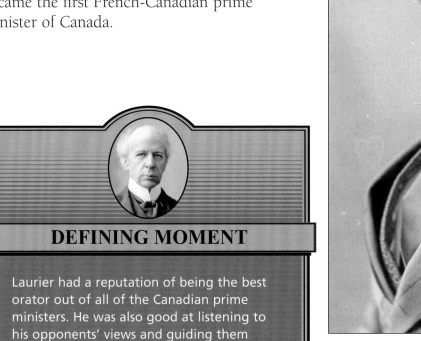

DEFINING MOMENT

Laurier had a reputation of being the best orator out of all of the Canadian prime ministers. He was also good at listening to his opponents' views and guiding them toward a compromise position.

During his days at the College de L'Assomption, a young Laurier became interested in politics and law.

Special People in Laurier's Life

> "I would rather be the wife of a simple [lawyer] in Arthabaska. It was the best time of my life."
>
> *Lady Laurier, in a letter to a friend, 1901*

The Diamond Jubilee attended by Laurier and Zoë was a celebration of Victoria's reign as Queen of England from 1837–1901.

Laurier met his future wife, Zoë Lafontaine, when he was a student. They lived in the same boarding house in Montreal. Zoë was a small, young woman with dark hair who dressed plainly. She supported herself by giving music and piano lessons. Their courtship began slowly. She played the piano in the evening, accompanying Laurier as he sang, reportedly, a little off key. Although Laurier was in love with Zoë, he secretly believed he was dying of tuberculosis. It would therefore be unfair to ask her to marry him, he thought. He left Montreal to set up his law practice in Arthabaska. Zoë was desperately unhappy because she loved Laurier. Her landlord was determined to bring the two young people together. He sent Laurier a telegram, that read "Come at once. A matter of urgent importance."

When Laurier arrived, his doctor told him that he had chronic bronchitis, not tuberculosis. The doctor said that as long as Laurier was careful, he would live a long life. Laurier then learned from Zoë's landlord that she loved him. They were married that same evening. Laurier and Zoë were married for 50 years, but they never had children.

When Laurier became an important politician, Zoë would accompany him on official occasions. A high point was when they both rode in the carriage behind Queen Victoria at the Diamond Jubilee celebrations in London.

In Ottawa, Zoë took an interest in politics and worked to improve her English. She became involved in a number of charities and was asked by Lady Aberdeen, the wife of the **governor general**, to serve as joint vice-president of the National Council of Women.

Two of the Laurier's closest friends were his law partner, Joseph Lavergne, and Joseph's wife, Emilie Lavergne. Laurier, Zoë, and Joseph first met Emilie at a garden party in Arthabaska. Joseph was captivated by this striking and intellectual woman who had travelled extensively and appeared very sophisticated. Emilie and Joseph Lavergne were married, and consequently Laurier frequently saw Emilie. He often sought her advice.

Lady Aberdeen was the wife of Canadian Governor General John Campbell Hamilton Gordon, officially titled the Marquess of Aberdeen and Temair.

French-Canadian Issues: The Manitoba Schools Question

> "Give our children the best education possible, put them on a footing of equality... and give them the legitimate pride which they will have in such a struggle. There is safety— there is autonomy."
>
> *Laurier, January 18, 1904*

The first issue Laurier had to deal with as prime minister was the Manitoba schools question. The Manitoba provincial government wanted to stop funding Catholic schools and to abolish French as an official language. The Conservative government was reluctant to act because French and English, and Catholics and Protestants across the country were bitterly divided on this issue.

Before he became prime minister, Laurier said, "If it was in my power, and if I had the responsibility, I would try the sunny way." In 1896, the voters decided to give Laurier a chance. Soon after winning the election, he reached a compromise agreement with Thomas Greenway, the **premier** of Manitoba. The two leaders agreed that religious instruction would be allowed for half an hour a day in the public schools. They also agreed that if there were enough children who spoke French, or any language other than English, then that school could provide bilingual instruction. French Canadians living in the West felt betrayed. Roman Catholics accused Laurier of giving in to English-Canadian Protestants. Laurier replied that this agreement was the best that could be hoped for, since Roman Catholics were in the minority in Manitoba.

The Manitoba schools question pitted English versus French and Catholics versus Protestants — common rivals throughout the turn of the 20th century.

Laurier Settles the West

"I think a stalwart peasant in a sheepskin coat, born on the soil whose forefathers have been farmers for ten generations, with a stout wife and a half dozen children is good quality. I am indifferent as to whether or not he is British born."

Clifford Sifton,
Laurier's minister in
charge of immigration

When Laurier came to power in 1896, there were not enough people to fill jobs created by the booming economy. There were not enough farmers to settle the vast tracts of land in the West. Laurier appointed Clifford Sifton to encourage immigration. Sifton realized that he needed to change people's ideas about Canada being a cold land. He had to inform them that Canada had plenty of fertile land and a suitable climate for farming.

Canadians had always thought of people from the British Isles, the United States, and western Europe as the ideal immigrants because they shared similar religious and cultural values. Now, Sifton turned his attention to people from other places, people such as the Galicians from Eastern Europe. He reasoned that they would be familiar with farming conditions on the Prairies and tough enough to handle the challenges they would face.

Sifton sent out agents across Europe. They gave talks about Canada and handed out pamphlets and brochures written in a variety of languages. The colourful illustrations and glowing reports about the land, climate, and advantages of moving to Canada encouraged more than 1 million immigrants to come to Canada between 1896 and 1905.

Life was hard for the newly arrived families. They had been attracted to Canada by the government's promise of free land, but when they saw the flat, empty prairies, with few trees and no neighbours close by, they began to worry.

The Changing Map of Canada

"So long as Canada remains a dependency of the British Crown the present powers that we have are not sufficient for the maintenance of our rights."

Laurier on the Alaska Boundary Dispute

When Laurier came to power, the map of Canada looked quite different from today. The increase in immigration led to the creation of Saskatchewan and Alberta in 1905. Under Laurier's leadership, the Yukon Territory was created, and the Alaska boundary was fixed.

In 1867, the United States bought Alaska from Russia. The United States would have liked British Columbia to become American too, but British Columbians joined Confederation in 1871. No one really knew where the boundary was between Alaska and Canada. When gold was found in the Yukon in 1897, Laurier's government quickly made it a separate territory. The United States and Canada could not agree on the boundary line between the Yukon and Alaska. To break the deadlock, a tribunal was created. The British judge on the tribunal sided with the United States against Canada. Canadians were very upset. Great Britain's decision convinced Laurier that Canada needed greater control over its own affairs.

In August 1910, Prime Minister Wilfrid Laurier drove the first spike into the Alberta Central Railway, which was to be a link in the new transcontinental railway. The link was later abandoned due to rising costs.

DEFINING MOMENT

The opening up of the Prairies produced bumper crops of wheat. The Canadian Pacific Railway could not keep up with the farm produce and goods that needed to be transported to and from the West. Laurier negotiated the construction of another transcontinental railway, the Grand Trunk Pacific Railway, from British Columbia to New Brunswick.

THE KLONDIKE GOLD RUSH

Between the spring of 1897 and the summer of 1899, the Klondike River in the Yukon Territory became the site of a gold-digging frenzy. Word of gold discovered in the Yukon spread quickly. Thousands of men and a few women rushed to make the hazardous trek up the Chilkoot Pass in search of fortune. A customs house sat at the top of the pass, where members of the North West Mounted Police prevented **prospectors** from travelling any farther unless they had enough supplies to last them for six months. Miners had to make repeated treks up the pass carrying heavy loads.

Once prospectors had all of their supplies at the top of the pass, there were another 800 kilometres to go before they reached the Klondike. More than 30,000 people made it to the gold fields, only to find most of the riverbeds had already been staked. In the summer of 1899, the prospectors left for Alaska and the next gold rush.

The Yukon Territory was rich with gold from the spring of 1897 to the summer of 1899.

DOUKHOBORS

The Doukhobors were a group of 7,400 Russian-speaking farmers who migrated to Canada in 1899. They had been persecuted in Russia for their religious beliefs. The Canadian government originally allowed them to settle together in communities on the Prairies. They were **pacifists** and believed in living a simple life of hard work and prayer. In 1905, they refused to swear an oath of allegiance and had to move from Saskatchewan to British Columbia.

HOME CHILDREN

The poverty in large British cities, such as London, Liverpool, and Glasgow, forced many families to place their children in orphanages. Between 1869 and 1930, some 100,000 of these children, called "Home Children," came to Canada to work on farms and as domestic servants.

Immigration Issues

The arrival of about two million people from around the world transformed the Canadian West into a society of many cultures. At first, Canadians welcomed these newcomers because they often took the hard jobs that no one else wanted. However, those immigrants who did not quickly learn Canadian customs and language soon began to have difficulties. African Americans were often stopped at the border and refused admission. African Americans in Oklahoma wanted to move to the Canadian West to take advantage of the cheap, fertile land advertised by the Canadian government. However, they discovered that Canada's "open-arms" policy did not apply to them. Government officials forbid African Americans entry because they were not suited to Canadian conditions and climate.

To help construct the Canadian Pacific Railway (CPR) through British Columbia, the government brought in more than 15,000 Chinese workers. Most of them were "pick and shovel" workers. It was dangerous work, and many died in the building of the railway. It is said that one worker died for every mile of track laid through the Rocky Mountains.

When the railway was complete, Chinese workers moved into jobs in mining, sawmills, fish canneries, and farming. This upset some Canadians who claimed there would be no jobs left for European immigrants and that Chinese-Canadians were causing wages to decrease because they were willing to work for very little money. The government responded to these grievances by imposing an entry fee, or "head tax," on Chinese immigrants. This practice began in 1885 when the tax was set at $50. The price was raised to $100 and then to $500 in 1903.

More than 15,000 workers were brought to Canada from China to work on the British Columbia section of the Canadian Pacific Railway. Nearly 600 died during construction.

Since this was the equivalent of two years' pay, only eight Chinese people arrived in Canada in 1904, in comparison to 5,000 the year before. Chinese immigration was prohibited entirely in 1923. It was not until after World War II, in 1947, that people of Chinese descent were again allowed to immigrate to Canada.

The British Columbia government took away Chinese Canadians' right to vote, and later passed laws prohibiting them from becoming doctors, lawyers, and pharmacists, and from working on government projects. Even cemeteries refused to accept Chinese corpses.

Gradually, some Chinese people moved eastward, where there were fewer restrictions on the kinds of jobs they could do. By 1901, there were 167 Chinese people in the Atlantic provinces, 1,044 in Quebec, 712 in Ontario, and 287 in the Prairies and the Territories. However, 14,376 Chinese people lived in British Columbia.

Laurier's government introduced an amendment to the Immigration Act that made it even more difficult for people to immigrate to Canada. The "continuous journey regulation" stated that all immigrants to Canada must come directly from their country of origin by a continuous journey on a ticket purchased in that country. This was an ingenious way of stopping immigration from India and Asia because the government knew that there was no direct steamship service from India to Canada. The act also prevented Japanese immigrants from getting around the immigration rules by arriving via Hawaii.

This regulation was tested in 1914, when the *Komagata Maru* steamship arrived in Vancouver harbour with 376 immigrants from India aboard. The men were not allowed to disembark and, for two months, the ship waited while the courts decided their fate. On July 23, HMCS *Rainbow* escorted the ship back out to sea, cheered on by local citizens.

The CPR joined Canada from sea to sea, making it easier to travel from one end of the country to the other.

DEFINING MOMENT

The Canadian government signed an agreement with the Japanese government to limit the number of Japanese immigrants each year. In 1907, hostility toward the Japanese resulted in a three-day riot in Vancouver. A crowd of about 7,000 broke windows and vandalized Japanese stores and houses. Laurier attempted to appease British Columbians of European and Japanese descent by limiting the immigration of Japanese to Canada to 400 per year. The victims were compensated for the damage to their property.

Worker Unrest:
The Cape Breton Coal Mines

"Business conditions compel us to very reluctantly ask for a reduction in wages."

E.P. Merril, general manager, to J.B. McLachlan, secretary-treasurer, District 26, concerning the wage cut for miners employed by the British Empire Steel Corporation in 1922

The booming Canadian economy was fuelled largely by coal dug in Cape Breton. The coal miners worked in dangerous conditions underground for 10 or more hours a day, 6 days a week. Accidents were common because of primitive conditions and lack of safety precautions. Coal companies dictated wages and owned the miners' houses and the stores where they shopped. Some men came home at the end of the month with virtually no wages left because their employer deducted most of their earnings for living expenses.

In 1909, many Cape Breton miners joined a **strike** organized by a new **union**, the United Mine Workers of America. The strike lasted almost 10 months. It was so violent that the government sent in 500 Canadian soldiers to settle the unrest. After several months with no pay and their families often starving and sick, the men went back to work. Their strike had failed.

Coal was an important natural resource to the Canadian economy at the turn of the 20th century.

Attitudes Toward Women Workers

By 1900, women made up a quarter of the manufacturing workforce. The largest number of women worked as domestic servants. These young women, many of whom were recent immigrants, spent their days cleaning other families' houses and looking after their children.

Housework was difficult. There were few labour-saving devices available. Laundry involved a great deal of heavy work. Water had to be heated and poured into tubs or wash boilers. The heavy, wet clothes had to be scrubbed and wrung out by hand and then dried on the line. In winter, damp laundry had to be hung inside around the stove to dry. Ironing clothing and linens was also time-consuming. Having to heat the irons on the stove made it hot and weary work in summer. The first electric washing machine was introduced in Canada in 1910. It needed to be filled and drained manually and tended to shred clothes.

Clerical and sales jobs were just beginning to open up for women because women were willing to work for lower wages. Women dominated the fields of teaching and nursing. Those occupations were thought to be part of a woman's role and therefore more suited to women than men.

At the turn of the century, three out of every four teachers were women. Female teachers were paid less than men, could not become principals, and were largely confined to elementary schools. However, women had begun to enter many of the professions that had been reserved for men. Almost one in ten university students was a woman.

In 1891, Carrie Derick was the first female professor in Canada. Cora Hind in Winnipeg and Kit Coleman in Toronto proved that women could be excellent journalists. Clara Martin succeeded in the legal profession. Women made slower progress in Quebec, where they were forbidden to practise law until 1941.

WOMEN IN SPORTS

Women who did well in athletics were considered unfeminine. Doctors stated that rigorous sports were harmful to female reproductive organs. However, by 1900, women were playing tennis, basketball, ice hockey, curling, and golf. Only games involving physical contact were completely closed to them.

Canadian Nationalism

Canadians fought under the flag of Great Britain in the Boer War of 1899 as a compromise made by Prime Minister Laurier.

THE SOUTH AFRICAN WAR

Laurier admired British traditions and institutions, but he was determined that Canada should be independent. In 1899, news arrived in Canada that Britain needed help in its war against Dutch settlers, also known as the Boers, in South Africa. Laurier's first response was to refuse. Canada had no interest in fighting the Boers, for whom French Canadians felt some sympathy. The Dutch settlers had been the first colonists in South Africa but had been conquered by the British in the same way that the French had been in Canada. English Canadians pressured Laurier to respond to Britain's call. His compromise was for Canada to pay for the recruitment and transportation of a battalion of volunteers to South Africa. Once they arrived, they would be paid by the British and would fight under the British flag.

The Canadian soldiers were poorly trained. Despite their inexperience, they were praised for their fighting spirit. Lieutenant E. W. B. Morrison commented that while, "Canada's soldiers ...lack to some extent the barrack yard polish...they more than make up for it in spirit and dash and a certain air of self-reliant readiness to hold their own."

THE NAVAL CRISIS

In 1910, there was growing fear in Britain that a war was looming in Europe. The British feared that the growing strength of Germany's navy was threatening British control of the high seas. The British Parliament asked Canada to help Britain prepare for war by contributing money to construct eight **dreadnought** battleships.

Laurier was again faced with a difficult task. If he offered Britain support, as English Canadians were insisting, then he would offend French Canadians who were against any involvement in a European war. French-Canadian **nationalists**, such as Henri Bourassa, cautioned that this would involve Canada in imperial and European wars in which Canada had no interest. Laurier's compromise was to introduce the Naval Service Bill. He proposed to create a Canadian navy whose warships could be loaned to Britain, if needed.

This time, his compromise did not work. French Canadians accused him of giving in to the British. English Canadians laughed at the "tin pot navy" that would be too small and too out of date to be of any help.

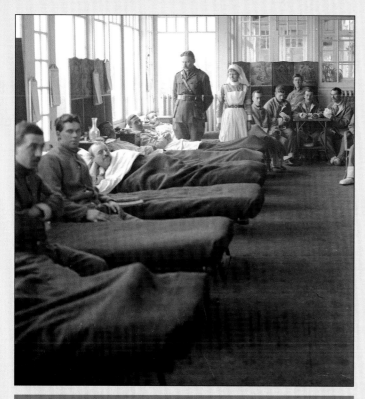

Canadian soldiers suffered from a lack of proper training in the Boer War, but were known for their excellent fighting spirit.

CONSCRIPTION RIOTS

When war broke out in 1914, Laurier was wholeheartedly in support of Britain. At first, even Henri Bourassa did not criticize the war because the Conservative government led by Robert Borden had promised there would be no **conscription**. However, many French Canadians questioned why Canada should take part in a war far away in Europe. When Prime Minister Borden decided, in 1917, that conscription must be introduced, the biggest outcry came from French Canadians.

Laurier, then the leader of the opposition, warned that conscription would be very unpopular. The archbishop of Montreal agreed and told Borden that he feared it would lead to revolt and bloodshed. Their warnings proved correct. When conscription was passed, there was a two-day riot in Montreal. Store windows

were broken, and rail lines were ripped up from the streets. Police were called in. Several people were wounded, and one demonstrator was killed. More rioting broke out later in Quebec City.

FRENCH CANADIANS

Henri Bourassa was a young, outspoken supporter of French-Canadian nationalism when Laurier asked him to run as a Liberal candidate in Quebec in the 1896 election. Bourassa was the grandson of Louis-Joseph Papineau, who had led the Patriotes in the 1837 **rebellion** in **Lower Canada**. Bourassa wanted to protect the language, customs, and religious rights of French Canadians. He became a star in Laurier's cabinet but resigned when Laurier agreed to send volunteers to the Boer War. Bourassa did not share Laurier's belief that compromise between French and English Canadians was necessary for the good of the nation. In 1907, Bourassa left politics and began a career as the publisher of *Le Devoir*, which is still one of the most important newspapers in Quebec.

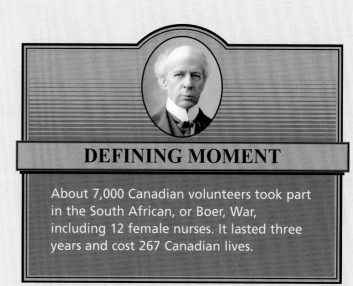

DEFINING MOMENT

About 7,000 Canadian volunteers took part in the South African, or Boer, War, including 12 female nurses. It lasted three years and cost 267 Canadian lives.

Laurier Falls from Power

"Our object today is to open the door of the American market, to open the door of a nation of 90,000,000, which has been closed to us for the last 50 years, and when we are now on the eve of reaching that long sought goal, we are met by objection after objection."

Laurier in the House of Commons, 1911

Laurier was Canada's prime minister for 15 years. During that time, Canada prospered and grew. Under Laurier's control, immigration expanded and settlers filled the Prairies. These immigrants created a huge market for goods manufactured in eastern Canada and produced large quantities of wheat for export. This expansion led to the creation of two provinces, a territory, and two railway lines.

In 1910, Laurier and his wife travelled to the new Prairie provinces and viewed for themselves the tremendous transformation that had taken place. At stops along the railway, Laurier spoke to the crowd. He listened as farmers told him their stories and their problems. They wanted free trade with the United States so they could sell their wheat and lumber at higher prices.

When Laurier called an election in 1911, he remembered their words and promised a **reciprocity** agreement with the U.S. government. It would provide special trade provisions to please the farmers, but it would not affect trade in manufactured goods. Laurier felt this would please business leaders, too. To Laurier's surprise, reciprocity was not popular with manufacturers. They feared it would take away business. Some Canadians accused Laurier of giving away Canada's economic and political independence to the Americans.

Laurier lost power in 1911 over the issue of reciprocity. Usually, a defeated party leader resigns after an election defeat, but Laurier kept his position and remained the leader of the opposition until his death in 1919.

The CPR allowed Laurier and others to travel across the vast Canadian land.

Laurier's Legacy

> "This cathedral is made of marble, oak and granite. It is the image of the nation I would like to see Canada become. For here, I want the marble to remain the marble; the granite to remain the granite; the oak to remain the oak; and out of all these elements I would build a nation great among the nations of the world."
>
> *Wilfrid Laurier*

When World War I began in 1914, Laurier supported Canada's war effort. However, he refused to support conscription in 1917, even though he knew most of his English-speaking Liberal members of Parliament would vote against him.

As he foresaw, in the election of that year, the Liberals won most of the seats in Quebec, but only 20 constituencies outside Quebec.

Even though Laurier was in his seventies, the split in the party seemed to energize him. He worked tirelessly after the war to mend the divisions between the French- and English-speaking Liberals.

Wilfrid Laurier died of a stroke at the age of 77 on February 17, 1919. He had been in politics for 45 years. The headline of the *Toronto Globe* next day read: "Canada's Greatest Son." The *Globe* called Laurier, "the exponent of the 'sunny ways,' the smile, the words of encouragement, the unfailing atmosphere of those things that make for happiness in life."

Laurier's funeral in Ottawa was attended by 100,000 people and hundreds of dignitaries from all regions of the country. Even ordinary citizens who had opposed his policies mourned his loss. Flags across the country were flown at half-mast. Buildings along the route of the funeral procession were draped in black and purple cloth to symbolize mourning.

Wilfrid Laurier served Canada as prime minister for 15 years, during which time Canada added two new provinces and a new territory.

Robert Laird Borden: Canada's War Leader

Prime Minister Robert Borden was the only allied leader to stay in office throughout the war.

Robert Laird Borden was born in Grant Pré, Nova Scotia, in 1854. In 1911, he became prime minister. Borden faced his most important challenge three years later when Canada joined Britain in the war against Germany and its allies. It was up to Borden to organize Canada's response. By the end of the war, Borden earned a greater voice for Canada in international affairs, a development that would later lead to greater independence from Britain.

Borden came from a farming family, but he did not like farming. He never enjoyed working on the fields, cutting wood, or doing any of the other farm chores. He preferred reading with his mother or studying classical poetry with his uncles. At school, he was a good student and worked hard. He thought that wasting time was "wasting one's future." Borden was ambitious. He wanted to be a lawyer.

He became an apprentice in a Halifax law firm. In 1877 he took the provincial bar examinations and finished at the top of his class. He began to move in political circles. He was asked to join the law firm of Charles Hibbert Tupper, the son of the future Conservative prime minister, Charles Tupper. Borden was a very successful lawyer, and his firm became one of the largest in Nova Scotia.

In April 1896, Charles Tupper asked Borden to stand for election. This was a major turning point in Borden's life. He won a seat in Halifax and split his time between his law practice in Halifax and his political duties in Ottawa. He was noticed as a fresh new face in the Conservative Party. To his amazement, he was asked to take over as leader after the defeat of the party in the 1900 election. He protested modestly, "I have not either the experience or the qualifications which would enable me to successfully lead the party...It would be an absurdity for the party and madness for me." Absurd or not, his colleagues persuaded him to become leader. He led his party for the next 19 years. A lawyer and a businessman, he never really enjoyed public speaking and, because of this, his political skills were sometimes doubted even by those in his own party.

Sir Charles Tupper became Canada's prime minister in 1896 and was in office only two months.

Courage, Patience, and Persistence

"Courage, patience, persistence and the saving grace of humour are perhaps the most useful qualities for one entering the lists of life."
Borden's speech to the graduating class at Acadia University in 1932

Special People in Borden's Life

> "I hereby give my consent—in your getting out of politics and—quick."
>
> *A note from Laura to Borden on how she felt about political life, February 4, 1906*

Borden met Laura Bond in the summer of 1886 when he was working in Halifax as a lawyer. Her father was a hardware merchant, and she sometimes played the organ at Saint Paul's Anglican Church. Laura and Robert had friends in common and shared a love of theatre and outdoor sports, particularly golf. They married in September 1889. The couple had no children, but they enjoyed the company of their dog, Taffy, and a cat named Lady Jane.

In 1916, Prime Minister Borden's office was badly damaged when a fire broke out at the Parliament buildings.

When Borden was first elected to Parliament, Laura remained at home in Halifax. Later, she accompanied him whenever Parliament was in session and enjoyed listening to the debates from the visitors' gallery of the **House of Commons**. However, she would have preferred her husband to return to his life as a successful lawyer. She did not enjoy the bickering and back-stabbing she experienced in Ottawa.

When Borden became prime minister, Laura had to move to Ottawa with her husband. After the war, Borden retired from politics. He and his wife spent many happy years together golfing, travelling, and doing charity work. She died on September 7, 1940. In his **memoirs**, Borden paid her this tribute: "In 1889 I had become engaged to be married to Laura Bond, whose devotion and helpfulness during all the succeeding years have been the chief support of my life's labours."

Eunice had a strong influence on her son. Borden admired his mother. He wrote that she had a "very strong character, remarkable energy, high ambition, and unusual ability." She was a strict disciplinarian and encouraged Robert and his brothers and sisters to work hard.

Borden's father was a widower with two children when he married Eunice Laird. Together, they had four children. Robert was the oldest, followed by a brother, John, and a sister, Julia. Borden's youngest brother, Henry, was known as Hal and became his favourite sibling. Borden was not very close to his father, although he considered him "a man of good ability and excellent judgment." Andrew Borden was station master at the Grand Pré stop on the Windsor and Annapolis Railway.

"Safety bicycles" became very popular in the 1890s.

DEFINING MOMENT

Borden took up the new fad of bicycling in the 1890s. The new "safety bicycle" had two equal-sized wheels driven by a chain, and inflatable tires, which were safer and more comfortable than the solid tires of earlier machines. These bikes could be ridden by anyone, and there was a subsequent boom in popularity. With his mane of white hair and bushy moustache, Borden was a noticeable figure when he cycled to work at Parliament Hill each day. He is said to have cycled 32 kilometres a day.

French-Canadian Issues: Conscription

When World War I broke out in Europe, Canada was part of the British Empire. Canada was automatically at war. At first, French and English Canadians were united in their determination to aid Great Britain and defeat the Axis powers of German and Austria-Hungary. Full of patriotism and sentiments of loyalty to the "Mother Country," thousands of Canadians flocked to sign up for service overseas. Many enlisted for the excitement, glory, and medals that they hoped would be theirs. Others joined for free room and board and $1 a day. Few people expected the war to last beyond Christmas.

After the initial burst of enthusiasm was over, French-Canadian support for the war waned. Unlike English Canadians, they had no ties with Britain. Although their roots were French, they had been in Canada for so many generations that they felt no attachment to France either.

French Canadians had another reason to be unsympathetic to the war effort. When French-Canadian men volunteered for service in Europe, they were often met with hostility. The recruiting stations were often staffed by English-speaking officers who did not want to work with French Canadians. The young French-Canadian recruits were often stationed in English-speaking regiments. They had no one to talk to and could not understand their orders.

As casualties mounted, it became more difficult to find replacements. Certain groups were less likely to enlist. French Canadians tended to view the war as merely another British imperial struggle. They preferred to work their farms rather than lose their lives on a distant battlefield in a war that had nothing to do with them.

Keeping Canada Together

"There has not been, there will not be, compulsion or conscription. Freely and voluntarily the manhood of Canada stands ready to fight beyond the seas in this quarrel for the Empire and its liberties."
Robert Borden

Workers objected to big business earning huge profits from the war, while they either died overseas or felt the pinch of rising inflation. Farmers resented losing their children when farming was essential to the war effort.

In the spring of 1917, Prime Minister Borden returned from the **front** determined to increase enlistments. He approached opposition leader Wilfrid Laurier about forming a **coalition** government to enforce conscription. When Laurier rejected this offer, Borden convinced many of Laurier's English-speaking MPs to join him in a coalition government called the Union Government. He called an election for December 17, 1917. The issue was simple—conscription or not.

To ensure victory, Borden granted the vote to women who had relatives fighting overseas. He took the vote away from German-speaking Canadians. The ensuing campaign brought out the worst in Canadian prejudices. The Laurier Liberals captured 62 of the 65 seats in Quebec, but only 20 constituencies outside Quebec. Borden won, but Canada was divided along French-English lines. Approximately 120,000 men were conscripted. The war ended earlier than the government expected. Of the 100,000 men called up, only 25,000 actually saw action.

The ill feeling caused by the conscription issue poisoned the relationship between English Canadians and French Canadians. French Canadians were more convinced than ever that their language and culture were in danger and that they must be vigilant to protect themselves against assimilation by English Canadians.

The political parties were also affected by the conscription crisis. The Liberal Party was left divided and weakened. Borden's Conservatives were strong with English Canadians but for many years were viewed with suspicion and dislike in Quebec.

The Canadian government used recruitment posters to convince young men to join the fight overseas.

CANADA'S ARMED FORCES

In 1914, Canada's armed forces consisted of an army of 3,100, a **militia** of some 60,000, and a navy of one light and one heavy cruiser. Thanks to enthusiastic enlistments, the army swelled to 250,000 in 1915, and to 500,000 the following year. By war's end, more than 600,000 men joined the army, with an additional 8,000 each for the navy and air force. Approximately 2,500 women served as nursing sisters overseas. More than 60,000 Canadians lost their lives, and another 173,000 were severely wounded or poisoned with chlorine gas.

The Battle of Vimy Ridge

> "A wonderful success. The grandest day the corps has ever had. The attack was carried out exactly as planned. The sight was awful and wonderful."
>
> *General Arthur Currie*

Filled with patriotic enthusiasm for "the war to end all wars," thousands of young Canadians were shipped to England for training. There, they spent three months **drilling** in the rain and mud. This did not prepare them for the terrible conditions that awaited them in the trenches of France.

By the spring of 1917, the Canadian Expeditionary Force had fought in every major battle, including the deadly Somme offensive. By this time, the Canadian public was losing faith in its leaders. The long lists of soldiers killed or injured in battles made people wonder whether the sacrifice of their sons, fathers, brothers, and husbands was worth it. Canadians read about rich businessmen making enormous profits by selling supplies to the army. They wondered why this was allowed, especially when they read about soldiers at the front suffering because of badly made equipment. When they heard that the officers commanding the war were sending troops "over the top" to certain death, they wondered why their political leaders let this continue.

A Canadian officer decided to do something to reduce casualties. When he was given the difficult task of taking an area called Vimy Ridge, General Arthur Currie decided to try a new approach. The Germans were sheltered in trenches and tunnels at the top of the ridge, which overlooked the countryside for miles around. Attackers would have to climb up the icy hill, breach rolls of barbed wire, and then avoid being shot down by German machine guns.

THE ROAD TO WAR

Summer of 1914

June 28
Archduke Ferdinand is assassinated at Sarajevo.

June 23
Austria-Hungary sends a list of demands to Serbia.

June 25
Serbia replies, rejecting one term.

June 28
Austria-Hungary declares war on Serbia.

August 1
Germany declares war on Russia.

August 3
France mobilizes forces to assist Russia. Germany declares war on France.

August 4
Britain declares war on Germany.

August 5
Canada and the rest of the British Empire are at war.

For the first time, Currie brought together all four units of the Canadian Expeditionary Force under Canadian leadership. For two months, he had them rehearse on a specially prepared area of ground modelled on the actual hill they were to conquer. They practised the "Vimy Glide"– moving up the hill at a timed speed that would keep them just behind a barrage of artillery fire that would disable the enemy guns and hide their approach. For the first time, soldiers were each given a map so that they could find their way if they became lost or separated from their comrades.

The practice paid off. It took four days, but the Canadians managed to dislodge the Germans and capture Vimy Ridge. Their heroic exploits gained international recognition for the contribution Canadians made to the war effort.

DEFINING MOMENT

In the spring of 1915, Canadian troops were stationed on the Western Front, near Ypres in Belgium. On the afternoon of April 22, 1915, a green cloud of chlorine gas slowly drifted over the area. French soldiers fled into the Canadian trenches. Most of them were blind and choking to death. They had been totally unprepared for this deadly new weapon. The Canadian troops managed to hold off the German attack. This won the Canadian army its first international recognition as a formidable fighting force. In just two weeks fighting at Ypres, there were 6,000 Canadian casualties, including 2,000 dead.

The Canadian Memorial at Vimy Ridge opened in 1936. The names of more than 11,000 Canadian soldiers who were killed in the battle are engraved on the monument's wall.

Calling all Canadians

"We see in the United States what grave problems may arise from the presence of a race unable to become full members of the same social family as ourselves."
Laurier, 1910

In Borden's time, the Canadian armed forces rarely accepted visible minorities. Some soldiers were unwilling to fight next to people unlike themselves. Army commanders argued that their units would not work as well if visible minorities were admitted. When visible minorities offered their services, they were turned down. Fifty African Canadians from Sydney, Nova Scotia, arrived at the recruitment office and were advised not to join.

Canada's visible minorities volunteered for battle out of a sense of patriotism and a yearning for adventure. They also believed that participation in the war would help improve the status of their culture. The government formed a African-Canadian labour battalion headquartered in Nova Scotia. More than 600 African Canadians served in the Canadian forces.

Units that were made up of visible minorities were segregated whenever possible from Canadians of European descent. African

On July 5, 1915, the Canadian government formed the Number 2 Construction Battalion for Canadians of African descent.

Canadians were segregated on ships and in camps. They had a separate YMCA for their evening entertainment. Their efforts were later largely forgotten in accounts of the war effort.

CANADA'S ABORIGINAL FIGHTERS

Many Canadian communities supported Canada's efforts in World War I. Canada's Aboriginal Peoples volunteered at twice the national average rate. At first, officials discouraged the recruitment of Aboriginal Canadians. Some felt that Aboriginals might be mistreated if they were captured. However, the need for men was great. About 4,000 Aboriginal Canadians fought in the war. They were greatly valued as scouts and snipers, two of the most dangerous and important combat positions. Canada's best snipers were Aboriginal Canadians. Henry "Ducky" Norwest, a Cree, had one of the best sharpshooting records in the British forces. Mike Mountain Horse, a member of the Blood Nation from Alberta, was awarded the Distinguished Conduct Medal for his actions at the Battle of Vimy Ridge. Only recently has the Canadian government created a special war memorial in Ottawa dedicated to the memory and contributions of Canada's Aboriginal fighters.

ENEMY AGENTS

When the war broke out, any resident in Canada who spoke an enemy language or had originally come from an enemy country was suspected of being an enemy agent. Approximately 500,000 Canadians had been born in Germany or Austria-Hungary, countries that had fought against Canada in World War I.

Stores owned by German-speaking people were attacked. The government banned all meetings and publications in "enemy" languages.

Henry "Ducky" Norwest, a former ranch hand and rodeo performer, was one of Canada's best snipers.

Hostility towards Germany was so strong that the town of Berlin, Ontario, changed its name to Kitchener. Descendants of Germans in Lunenburg, Nova Scotia, claimed to be Dutch.

People classified as enemy agents were closely watched. Those considered dangerous were either sent to **internment camps** or forced to carry identity cards and report regularly to the authorities. Approximately 8,300 enemy agents were detained in 24 camps set up throughout Canada.

JEREMIAH JONES

Jeremiah Jones was an African Canadian who fought bravely at Vimy Ridge. He was known as the "Friendly Giant." Jones, at the age of fifty-six, stormed across the ridge and seized an enemy machine gun nest by himself. "I threw a hand bomb right into the nest and killed about seven of them," he reported. The survivors surrendered to Jones. His commanding officer wanted to award him the Distinguished Conduct Medal, the second highest award for valour. However, because Jones was an African Canadian, he was not given the medal.

Canada's Place in the World

> "The great dominions, sharing in the defence of the Empire upon the high seas, must necessarily be entitled to share also in the responsibility for and in the control of foreign policy."
>
> *Borden speaking to British leaders during the war*

Borden was an **imperialist**. He had often criticized Laurier's reluctance to give in to British demands. He was also a Canadian nationalist. When he became prime minister, he realized Laurier had been right to insist that Canada should have an independent position within the British Empire. If Canada was going to lend its ships and send soldiers to Britain, Canadian leaders should have a say in how they were used. Borden was infuriated when the British brushed off his requests for more information and only shared with him news he could find in the daily papers.

Borden believed that Canada's important role and sacrifices in the war had demonstrated that Canadians deserved more say in imperial policy. He wanted the Dominions of the British Empire—Canada, Australia, New Zealand, and South Africa—to have power in proportion to their military contribution to the war. When a new prime minister was elected in Britain, things began to change. David Lloyd George invited Borden and other Dominion leaders to form an Imperial War Cabinet and hold regular conferences. Resolution IX recognized the independence of the Dominions within the British Commonwealth and the need for them to be regularly consulted.

Growing Canadian independence was further demonstrated when Borden was given a seat at the Paris Peace Conference in 1919. Canada signed the Treaty of Versailles, which officially ended the war. Borden also fought for a seat for Canada on the new League of Nations, which was formed to prevent the outbreak of future wars.

On behalf of Canada, Borden signed the Treaty of Versailles at the Paris Peace Conference.

Women's Issues: Gaining the Vote

Women had been demanding the right to vote in political elections since the 1880s. World War I was the catalyst that persuaded politicians to give it to them. The breakthrough came first in Manitoba, the home of well-known suffrage reformer Nellie McClung. She was an entertaining speaker who used humour to persuade her audience.

On January 28, 1916, Manitoba became the first province to allow women to vote in provincial elections and to stand for elected office. The other western provinces quickly followed. Soon, every province except Quebec granted women the vote.

Prime Minister Borden had supported women's suffrage in the past. Now, because he wanted to introduce conscription, he passed the Wartime Elections Act on September 20, 1917. The Act gave the vote to the wives, mothers, and sisters of soldiers, as well as to women serving in the armed forces. This was interpreted by many Canadians as fixing the election. His gamble paid off, and his coalition government was easily elected.

In 1918, all women over 21 years of age were allowed to vote in federal elections. Aboriginal and Asian women were excluded. For the first time, a woman, Agnes Macphail, was elected to the House of Commons.

"Our worthy opponents will emphasize the fact that women are the weaker vessel. Well I should think that a woman who cooks for men, washes and bakes and scrubs and sews for her family could stand the extra strain of marking a ballot every four years."
Nellie McClung

Nellie McClung gave fiery speeches in favour of women having the right to vote.

Medical Issues: The Spanish Flu

"It is not the return home that I had dreamed of…it seems to me that my life will always be empty now. My God, if it was to know such suffering upon my return why did I not die at the front, killed by a bullet?"

Lieutenant Arthur-Joseph Lapointe on arriving home to the news that five of his siblings had died in nine days

Canadians celebrated the end of the war with street parties and parades, but unknown to them, a new disaster was already looming. The Spanish influenza virus swept through the civilian population. Before it was over, almost as many Canadians died from the flu as those who were killed on the battlefields of Europe.

The Spanish flu started in China and quickly spread to Canada. It struck down even the young and healthy. Almost every family lost members to the flu. It infected one in four Canadians. Even those who did not die from the flu were left weak and susceptible to other deadly infections such as pneumonia. Nearly 50,000 Canadians died as a result of the flu. To try to deal with the **pandemic**, Borden created the first national Department of Health in 1919.

Doctors could do little to stop the Spanish flu from spreading. At the height of the pandemic, many Canadians wore masks to protect themselves from the airborne virus. Some even tried home remedies, such as wearing smoked herrings around their necks or eating garlic and raw onions. Schools, businesses, and public buildings closed to avoid spreading the disease. Hospitals were overflowing. Returning soldiers sometimes passed it on to their families, friends, and neighbours. Men who had seen their comrades die in battle sometimes came home to find their families wiped out by the illness. The Spanish flu killed more than 20 million people around the world and remained active until the mid-1920s.

People wore masks over their noses and mouths to protect themselves from the influenza virus during the 1918–1919 outbreak.

Labour Issues:
The Winnipeg General Strike

Prime Minister Borden had given little thought to what would happen after the war was over. Returning soldiers came home to find factories closing down, prices rising, **bankruptcies**, and **unemployment**. This was not the better world they had been fighting for.

On May 15, 1919, more than 30,000 discontented war veterans and other workers walked off their jobs in Winnipeg in support of striking building and metal workers. This was Canada's first general strike. The workers demanded more jobs, higher wages, and better working conditions. It was the largest workers' revolt in Canadian history. Business leaders in Winnipeg accused the strikers of being **revolutionaries.**

The government and employers tried to stop the strike. **Federal government** employees were told to go back to work or they would be fired. The Immigration Act was changed so that immigrants could be deported more easily. Union leaders were arrested. Labour publications were banned. The mayor of Winnipeg brought in the Royal Canadian Mounted Police and hired several hundred special constables to keep order.

On June 21, war veterans organized a protest parade, and a crowd of 6,000 people gathered in support. A streetcar full of strikebreakers was overturned and set on fire. The Mounties and the "Specials" charged into the crowd, and a riot broke out. Two strikers were killed, 34 others were wounded, and 94 people were arrested. As a result of "Bloody Saturday," the strikers returned to work.

> "[How dare you] ask a man to go out and risk his life and when he returns, calmly request him to hand in his uniform, and in exchange hand him a pittance that will reduce a once self-respecting citizen to a miserable pauper, dependent on either charity or friends"
>
> *Helen Armstrong, leader of the strikers' wives*

On June 21, 1919, an organized protest became a riot on the streets of Winnipeg, Manitoba. This day is known as Bloody Sunday.

Borden Retires

> "There is nothing that oppresses me. Books, some business avocation, my wild garden, the birds and the flowers, a little golf, and a great deal of life in the open – these together make up the fullness of my days."
>
> *Borden speaking about retirement*

All his life, Borden suffered from periods of illness due to overwork. The war took an enormous toll on his mental and physical health, and led to his resignation in 1920. His good luck charm as a politician was a "lucky sprig." It was a shamrock that had been presented to him for luck during the 1911 election campaign. He carried it in his pocket book throughout that election and then again in 1917. He also took it to Europe with him the following year. Borden passed it on to his successor, Arthur Meighen. It did not work for Meighen, who lost the 1921 election.

After leaving politics, Borden became active in a variety of business concerns. He also acted as a **diplomat**, university **chancellor**, author, and lecturer. Some of his lectures about the Canadian Constitution were published. He even found time to write his memoirs. He and Laura were wealthy and continued to live at Glensmere, where they regularly entertained friends. Borden particularly enjoyed golfing and working in his wildflower garden on the banks of the Rideau River. He died of heart failure at the age of 82 on June 10, 1937.

Robert Borden never had the magnetic charm of Wilfrid Laurier, but he had a strong sense of duty and responsibility. It drove him to do his best for the country. His visits to the Canadian soldiers on the front lines during the war fired him with a sense of urgency and the need to do whatever he could to support them. He never forgot the soldiers who had fought in World War I, and they never forgot him. A thousand war veterans lined his funeral route in Ottawa. In his will, Borden left a trust fund so that a wreath would be laid at the National War Memorial each year.

The National War Memorial is located in Ottawa, the capital city of Canada.

Borden's Legacy

Under Borden, Canada increased its international stature. Canada made a notable contribution to the allied war effort. With a population of only 8 million, 600,000 Canadian troops were sent to fight in Europe. This was a greater proportion than any other British **colony**. It enabled Borden to demand that Canada have a greater voice in imperial affairs, a role at the Versailles peace talks, and a seat at the League of Nations.

One of the measures Borden took to finance the war was the introduction of the first income tax. This did not cause much controversy at the time, and in the future, it provided an enormously significant income for the federal government. Other initiatives he undertook were the nationalization of bankrupt railways, the introduction of veterans' benefits, the establishment of daylight savings time, and the replacement of traditional **patronage** by a professional civil service.

The most divisive issue Borden dealt with was conscription. The Conservative Party lost support from eastern European immigrants and French Canadians as a result.

One of the most notable legacies of the Borden administration was the right for Canadian women to vote in federal elections and stand for office. The only exception was Quebec, where women did not gain the vote until 1940.

> "Never once did Borden conceive of Canada as a subordinate or colonial participant in the war: Canada was fighting in her own right, though Britain had often to be reminded of it. This theme ran through the whole of Borden's wartime policy…"
>
> *Historians Robert Craig Brown and Ramsay Cook about Borden's retirement*

As prime minister, Borden allowed Canadian women the right to vote and hold office.

Timeline

1840s	1850s	1860s	1870s
PRIME MINISTERS			
Laurier is born on November 20, 1841.	Borden is born on June 26, 1854.	Borden attends Acadia Villa Academy. He is promoted to assistant master in 1869. Laurier begins his career as a lawyer and courts Zoë Lafontaine.	Laurier enters political life. Borden becomes a law student in Halifax.
CANADA			
Upper and Lower Canada are united in 1841.	Railway mania sweeps through the colonies. There is a gold rush in Yukon Territory.	Confederation takes place in 1867. Canada buys the Northwest Territories from the Hudson's Bay Company in 1869.	British Columbia becomes a province in 1871. Prince Edward Island joins Confederation in 1873.
WORLD			
Charles Dickens publishes *A Christmas Carol* in 1843. There is a famine in Ireland due to potato blight. More than 300,000 Irish immigrate to **British North America**.	Revolutions take place in France, Austria-Hungary, Italy, and Germany.	In 1865, Louis Pasteur publishes his theory that germs spread disease.	In 1871, P. T. Barnum opens a circus, calling it "The Greatest Show on Earth."

1880s | 1890s | 1900s

PRIME MINISTERS

Borden is invited to join a prestigious Halifax law firm. He marries Laura Bond in 1889.

Laurier becomes leader of the Liberal Party and wins the 1896 election.

Laurier settles the Manitoba schools question.

Borden plays a leading role in organizing the founding of Canadian Bar Association in 1896. He wins the Halifax seat in the 1896 election.

Borden heads the Conservative Party. He is the leader of the opposition from 1901–1911.

Laurier sends volunteers to fight in South Africa.

CANADA

Louis Riél is hanged in 1885.

In 1880, Calixa Lavallee writes Canada's national anthem.

James Naismith invents basketball in 1881.

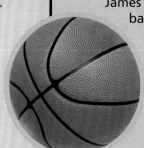

Alberta and Saskatchewan become provinces in 1905.

L. M. Montgomery publishes *Anne of Green Gables* in 1908.

WORLD

Karl Marx dies in 1883.

Thomas Edison invents the first light bulb for practical home use.

Thomas Edison invents the motion picture in 1891.

Queen Victoria dies in 1901.

In 1903, the Wright Brothers fly the first airplane.

Did You Know?

The first time a large group of Canadian soldiers served overseas was during the South African, or Boer, War. One of the volunteers was John McCrae. He became famous for his poem, *In Flanders Fields*.

Sir Robert Borden was the last prime minister to accept a knighthood and the first to attend a British Cabinet meeting.

Wilfrid Laurier's funeral was one of the first public events to be filmed in Canada.

In 1927, Wilfrid Laurier and John A. Macdonald were the first prime ministers to be represented on a stamp. In 1935, they were also the first leaders whose portraits appeared on bank notes. Macdonald was represented on the $500 note, and Laurier's face was on the $1,000 note. Robert Borden was represented on a stamp in 1973, and on a $100 bank note in 1969.

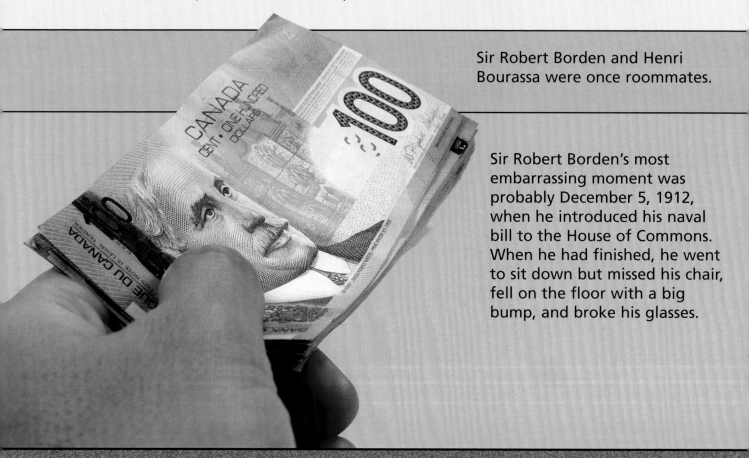

Sir Robert Borden and Henri Bourassa were once roommates.

Sir Robert Borden's most embarrassing moment was probably December 5, 1912, when he introduced his naval bill to the House of Commons. When he had finished, he went to sit down but missed his chair, fell on the floor with a big bump, and broke his glasses.

Test Your Knowledge

Multiple:

Where did Wilfrid Laurier grow up?

A) Halifax, Nova Scotia
B) Saint-Lin, Quebec
C) Montreal, Quebec

B) Saint-Lin, Quebec

Question:

Is the following statement true or false?

Wilfrid Laurier was the first French-Canadian prime minister.

true

Multiple:

To what political party did Robert Borden belong?

A) Conservative Party
B) Liberal Party
C) New Democratic Party

A) Conservative Party

Multiple:

What is Wilfrid Laurier's wife's name?

A) Laura Bond
B) Zoë Lafontaine
C) Nellie McClung

B) Zoë Lafontaine

Question:

Which Canadian prime minister supported and eventually enforced conscription?

Robert Borden

Question:

In what year was Chinese immigration prohibited entirely?

1923

Question:

When was the Klondike Gold Rush?

Between the spring of 1897 and the summer of 1899

Question:

Which Canadian prime minister was the first to attend a British Cabinet meeting?

Robert Borden

Question:

During World War I, who was one of the record-holding sharpshooters in the British forces?

Henry "Ducky" Norwest

Activity

Every day we are subjected to propaganda. Advertisements cleverly try to convince Canadians to buy a particular brand of shoe or soft drink. Wars create the most propaganda. Each country uses propaganda as part of its military strategy. At the home front, messages are created to instill pride in the country's war effort, to build confidence, and to inspire sacrifice. Other propaganda is designed to boost the morale of soldiers.

As World War I dragged on and casualties mounted, Robert Borden's Conservative government began an extensive propaganda campaign designed to bolster morale and convince Canadians of their responsibility to contribute their time, energy, and money to the war effort. Posters, songs, poems, fiction, and cartoons were essential elements in this program.

THE TORCH: BE YOURS TO HOLD IT HIGH!
IF YE BREAK FAITH WITH US WHO DIE
WE SHALL NOT SLEEP, THOUGH POPPIES GROW
IN FLANDERS FIELDS.
McCREA.

ANALYZING PROPAGANDA

To analyze propaganda, ask these questions about the document:

Who made it?

When was it created?

For whom was it designed?

What was its purpose?

What emotions were being appealed to?

Analyze the poster on this page using these questions. Create a suitable poster that contains similar themes. At the bottom of your poster, discuss how it was designed to achieve its goal.

For examples of other propaganda posters, visit: www.firstworldwar.com/posters/canada.htm

Further Research

Books

To find out more about Canadian prime ministers, visit your local library. Most libraries have computers that connect to a database for researching information. If you input a key word, you will be provided with a list of books in the library that contain information on that topic. Non-fiction books are arranged numerically, using their call number. Fiction books are organized alphabetically by the author's last name.

Websites

The World Wide Web is also a good source of information. Reputable websites usually include government sites, educational sites, and online encyclopedias. Visit the following sites to learn more about Canadian prime ministers.

Watch the map of Canada be transformed over time on Canadian Geographic's website.
www.canadiangeographic.ca/mapping/mappingcanada/default.html

Read first-hand accounts of Canadians during World War I on a Canadian government website.
www.collectionscanada.ca/firstworldwar/index-e.html

Watch the video of Wilfrid Laurier's funeral on Collections Canada's website.
http://collectionscanada.ca/primeministers/h4-2415-e.html

Visit an interactive site featuring every Canadian prime minister from John A. Macdonald to Stephen Harper.
www.primeministers.ca/index.php

Glossary

bankruptcies: when businesses or individuals have no money and are unable to pay their debts

charismatic: magnetic and compelling personal power

conscription: when people are forced by law to join the armed forces during wartime

dreadnought: a heavily armed and armoured battleship

drilling: military training

front: the foremost line of troops during wartime

immigrants: people who come into a country or region to live

internment camps: large camps where people who are thought to be possible enemies are held

memoirs: an autobiography

militia: an army of civilians who are not regular soldiers, but who undergo training for emergency duty or nation defence

nationalists: people who have great pride in their country

pacifists: people who are opposed to war and support peace

pandemic: a disease affecting a large number of people in a large part of the world

patronage: the power to give jobs or favours in return for political support

prospectors: people who search a region for gold

reciprocity: in the 19th century, the term broadly used for free trade

strike: an act of protest when workers refuse to work in order to get more pay, shorter hours, or improved working conditions

textiles: woven or knit fabrics

unemployment: the state of being without a job

union: an organized group of workers that campaigns for the rights of its members

Political Terms

British North America: after the United States broke away from Britain, the remaining British colonies in North America were together called British North America

chancellor: a high official within a university

civil service: people who work for the administration of the government

coalition: when two or more opposing groups agree to work together

colony: a region ruled by a country that is usually far away

Confederation: the event in 1867 when Canada became its own country

diplomat: someone who represents his or her country overseas

federal government: the government of the country, as opposed to provincial or municipal governments

governor general: the representative of the British monarch in Canada

House of Commons: people who have been elected from across Canada to make laws for the whole country

imperialist: a person who favours the policy of extending the authority of one country over other countries and territories

Lower Canada: mostly French-speaking colony created by Great Britain in 1791, re-named Canada East in 1841 when it united with Upper Canada (Canada West) to form the United Province of Canada. Today, Lower Canada is known as Quebec.

Parliament: the House of Commons and the Senate

premier: a Canadian province's head of government

rebellion: a revolt against the government that is in power.

revolutionaries: people who want to use violence to overthrow the state

Index